To My Cool Cousin:

All boys love Easter
bunnies, chocolate, egg hunts, and
a basket full of wonderful things!

I hope Easter is egg-citing...
filled with fun and adventure for
my COOL COUSIN!

A boy as special as you
should get your favorite
goodies from the Easter bunny!

Here's wishing the Easter Bunny brings you the best and most colorful eggs!

HOP! HOP! HOP! The Easter
Bunny is on his way to make sure
you have plenty of sweet treats!

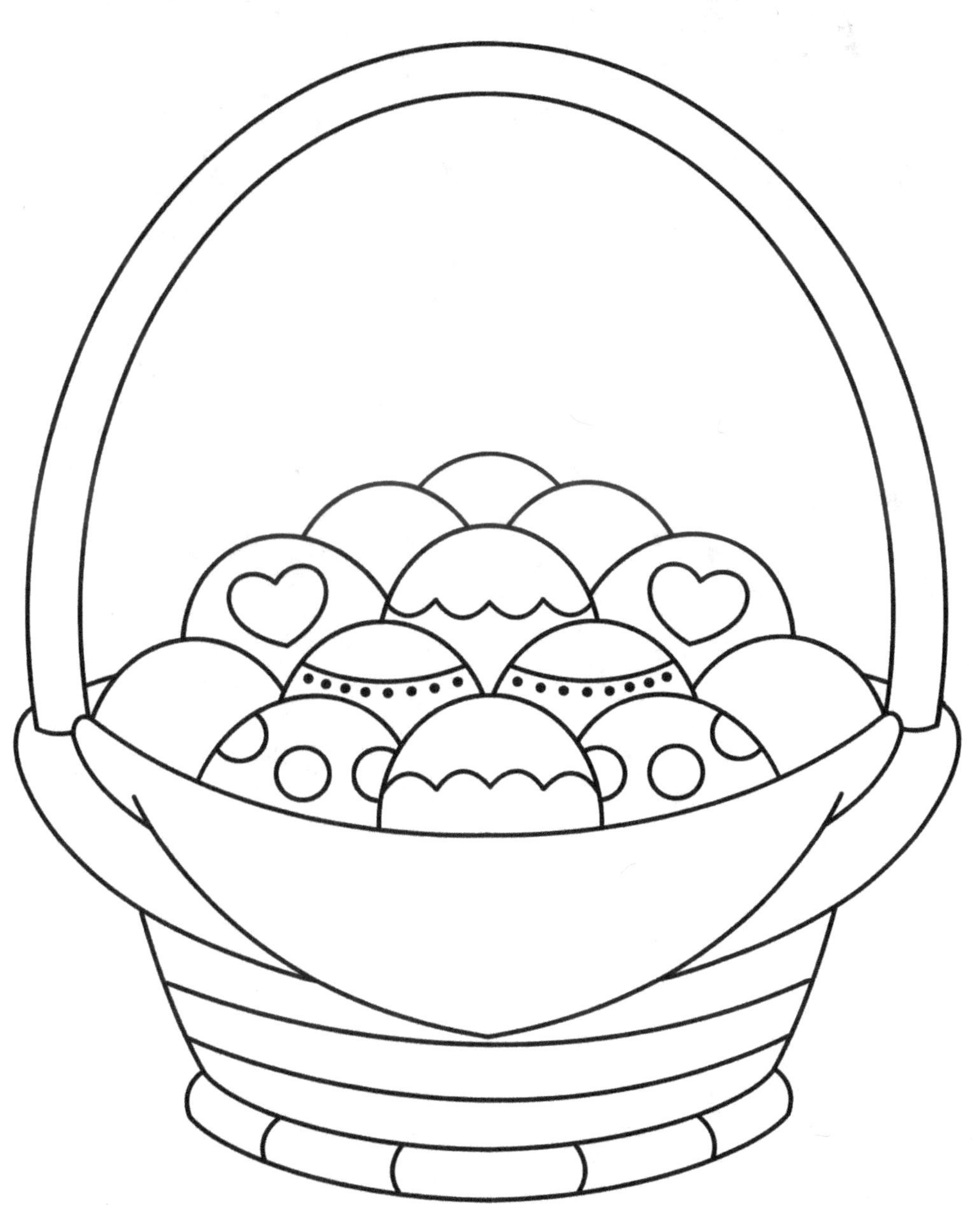

Wishing you a wonderful time as you celebrate Easter with family & friends!

One of the best things about Easter is...
all of the chocolate eggs
boys get to eat!

The Easter Bunny told me that you
are an EGG-STRA
COOL COUSIN!

There is no other boy in the world that deserves more fun than you this Easter!

Have a fantastic Easter with plenty of
chirping chickens & fluffy bunnies!

Good luck this year on your
Easter egg hunt!

Happy Easter
To My COOL COUSIN!
(Coloring Card)
(Personalized Card) Easter Messages,
Wishes, & Greetings for Children!

May you have a wonderful
holiday and your basket is filled with
lots of holiday things.